ALL AROUND THE WORLD
ROMANIA

by Kristine Spanier, MLIS

pogo

Ideas for Parents and Teachers

Pogo Books let children practice reading informational text while introducing them to nonfiction features such as headings, labels, sidebars, maps, and diagrams, as well as a table of contents, glossary, and index.

Carefully leveled text with a strong photo match offers early fluent readers the support they need to succeed.

Before Reading

- "Walk" through the book and point out the various nonfiction features. Ask the student what purpose each feature serves.
- Look at the glossary together. Read and discuss the words.

Read the Book

- Have the child read the book independently.
- Invite him or her to list questions that arise from reading.

After Reading

- Discuss the child's questions. Talk about how he or she might find answers to those questions.
- Prompt the child to think more. Ask: Romanian castles have inspired authors to write books about them. Have you read books that take place in castles? Would you like to?

Pogo Books are published by Jump!
5357 Penn Avenue South
Minneapolis, MN 55419
www.jumplibrary.com

Copyright © 2023 Jump!
International copyright reserved in all countries. No part of this book may be reproduced in any form without written permission from the publisher.

Library of Congress Cataloging-in-Publication Data

Names: Spanier, Kristine, author.
Title: Romania / by Kristine Spanier, MLIS.
Description: Minneapolis, MN: Jump!, Inc., [2023]
Series: All around the world | Includes index.
Audience: Ages 7-10
Identifiers: LCCN 2022026029 (print)
LCCN 2022026030 (ebook)
ISBN 9798885242066 (hardcover)
ISBN 9798885242073 (paperback)
ISBN 9798885242080 (ebook)
Subjects: LCSH: Romania–Juvenile literature.
Classification: LCC DR205 .S58 2023 (print)
LCC DR205 (ebook)
DDC 949.8–dc23/eng/20220608
LC record available at https://lccn.loc.gov/2022026029
LC ebook record available at https://lccn.loc.gov/2022026030

Editor: Jenna Gleisner
Designer: Molly Ballanger

Photo Credits: SCStock/Shutterstock, cover; Dragosh Co/Shutterstock, 1; Pixfiction/Shutterstock, 3; ANAND RAVEENDRAN/Shutterstock, 4; Andrew Mayovskyy/Shutterstock, 5; Calin Stan/Shutterstock, 6-7; Calin Stan/iStock, 8-9; F8 studio/Shutterstock, 10; Jaap Arriens/NurPhoto/Getty, 11; Ioan Panaite/Shutterstock, 12-13; JackF/iStock, 14; Gaspar Janos/Shutterstock, 15; Nic Vilceanu/Shutterstock, 16; marchevcabogdan/Shutterstock, 16-17; ELEPHOTOS/Shutterstock, 18-19; Robertus Pudyanto/Getty, 20-21; Diegobib/Dreamstime, 23.

Printed in the United States of America at Corporate Graphics in North Mankato, Minnesota.

TABLE OF CONTENTS

CHAPTER 1
Castles and Kings 4

CHAPTER 2
Capital City 10

CHAPTER 3
Life in Romania 14

QUICK FACTS & TOOLS
At a Glance 22
Glossary 23
Index 24
To Learn More 24

CHAPTER 1
CASTLES AND KINGS

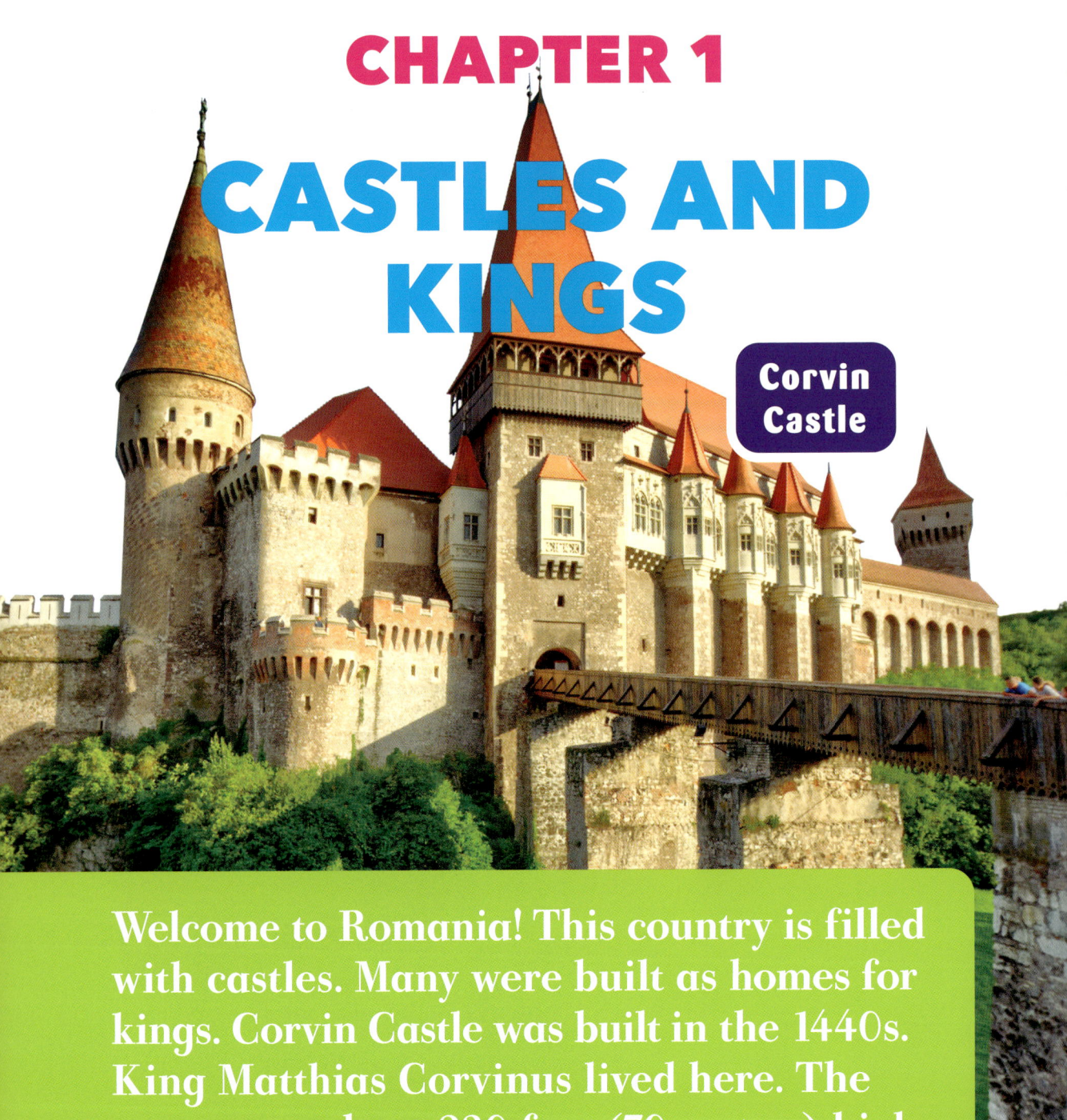

Corvin Castle

Welcome to Romania! This country is filled with castles. Many were built as homes for kings. Corvin Castle was built in the 1440s. King Matthias Corvinus lived here. The towers are about 230 feet (70 meters) high.

Bran Castle

Some say the vampire Count Dracula once lived in Bran Castle. But he is not real. He is a character in a book. Bran Castle is in Transylvania. This **region** is in central Romania.

Romania is in southeastern Europe. The Black Sea is east. The Danube River flows along the southern border. A carving of King Decebalus is along the river. He was king almost 2,000 years ago. The carving is more than 130 feet (40 m) high.

CHAPTER 1 7

The Carpathian Mountains run through the country. Peles Castle is nestled in them. This castle was built for King Carol I. It was a home for royalty until 1947.

DID YOU KNOW?

The country's tallest point is Moldoveanu Peak. It is in the Southern Carpathians. It is 8,346 feet (2,544 m) tall.

CHAPTER 2
CAPITAL CITY

Bucharest is the **capital**. Almost 2 million people live here. The Dambovita River flows through the city.

Bucharest

Romanians can vote at age 18. They **elect** a president.

ballot

CHAPTER 2 11

People also elect members of **parliament**. This group makes laws. It meets in the Palace of Parliament. This is the second-largest government building in the world! More than 100,000 workers helped build it.

WHAT DO YOU THINK?

Romania joined the **North Atlantic Treaty Organization (NATO)** in 2004. It joined the **European Union (EU)** in 2007. These groups work to protect the freedom of countries that belong to them. Do you think countries are stronger working together? Why?

Palace of Parliament

CHAPTER 2 · 13

CHAPTER 3
LIFE IN ROMANIA

Students learn at least two other languages in addition to Romanian. Most choose between English, French, Spanish, German, and Italian.

Many people in Romania have **service jobs**. Vehicle **manufacturing** is an important **industry**, too. Farmers raise sheep and cattle. They grow **crops** like corn, peas, potatoes, and cabbage.

corn

Crops are used to make many foods. Cabbage rolls are filled with pork, bacon, and rice. Mamaliga is the national dish. It is cornmeal porridge. Cozonac is a holiday sweet bread. It is flavored with orange and lemon. It has a nut filling.

WHAT DO YOU THINK?

Preparing family recipes is one way to remember one's **heritage**. Do you think it is important to remember family history? Why or why not?

cozonac

CHAPTER 3

Folk festivals take place around the country. People dress in **traditional** clothing. They dance to music that is hundreds of years old. Together, they enjoy Romanian food.

TAKE A LOOK!

Traditional clothing looks different depending on where people are from in Romania. But the outfits all have a lot in common. Take a look!

- VEST
- BLOUSE
- APRON
- LONG SHIRT
- SKIRT
- PANTS

People have fun all year in Romania. In summer, they play oina. This sport is like baseball. Soccer and tennis are popular sports, too. In winter, people ski in the mountains.

There is a lot to do in Romania. Do you want to visit?

QUICK FACTS & TOOLS

AT A GLANCE

ROMANIA

Location: southeastern Europe

Size: 92,043 square miles (238,390 square kilometers)

Population: 18,519,899 (2022 estimate)

Capital: Bucharest

Type of Government: semi-presidential republic

Languages: Romanian (official), Hungarian, Romani

Exports: cars and vehicle parts, electrical equipment, petroleum

Currency: Romanian leu

GLOSSARY

capital: A city where government leaders meet.

crops: Plants grown for food.

elect: To choose someone by voting for him or her.

European Union (EU): A group of European countries that have joined together to encourage economic and political cooperation.

folk: Traditional and belonging to the common people in a region.

heritage: Traditions and beliefs that a family, country, or society considers an important part of its history.

industry: A branch of business or trade.

manufacturing: The industry of making something on a large scale using special equipment or machinery.

North Atlantic Treaty Organization (NATO): An organization of countries that have agreed to give each other military help. This group includes the United States, Canada, and some countries in Europe.

parliament: A group of people elected to make laws.

region: A general area or specific district or territory.

service jobs: Jobs and work that provide services for others, such as hotel, restaurant, and retail positions.

traditional: Having to do with the customs, beliefs, or activities that are handed down from one generation to the next.

Romania's currency

INDEX

Black Sea 7
Bran Castle 5
Bucharest 10
Carpathian Mountains 8
clothing 18, 19
Corvin Castle 4
crops 15, 16
Dambovita River 10
Danube River 7
European Union 12
folk festivals 18
foods 16, 18
kings 4, 7, 8
languages 14
manufacturing 15
Moldoveanu Peak 8
North Atlantic Treaty Organization 12
Palace of Parliament 12
parliament 12
Peles Castle 8
president 11
service jobs 15
sports 21
students 14
Transylvania 5
vote 11

TO LEARN MORE

Finding more information is as easy as 1, 2, 3.
1. Go to www.factsurfer.com
2. Enter "Romania" into the search box.
3. Choose your book to see a list of websites.